Easiest Mandolin Tunes for Children

by Larry McCabe

Online Audio www.melbay.com/21246BCDEB

Audio Contents

1	Tuning Notes	13	Cripple Creek
2	Sweet Betsy from Pike	14	Sally Goodin
3	John Hardy	15	Groundhog
4	Sweet Sunny South	16	Brigg's Jig
5	Reuben and Rachel	17	Steamboat Waltz
6	Jack of Diamonds	18	Fire on the Mountain
7	Boil the Cabbage Down	19	Molly Put the Kettle On
8	Salty Dog Blues	20	New River Train
9	Black-Eyed Suzie	21	Red Haired Boy
10	Colinda	22	Angeline the Baker
11	Eighth of January, The	23	White Cockade, The
12	Shortnin' Bread	24	Watermelon on the Vine

MEL BAY®

1 2 3 4 5 6 7 8 9 0

Visit us on the Web at www.melbay.com — E-mail us at email@melbay.com

CONTENTS

HOW TO USE THIS BOOK

This book can be used by all beginning and early intermediate mandolin players; no prior playing experience or note reading ability is required.

The Tunes

Each mandolin tune is written in standard notation and *tablature.* Tablature allows the player to learn tunes even if s/he does know how to read music. The tablature staff (which is located underneath the music staff) shows the *string and finger position* of each note. Learning how to read tablature (page 8) is a simple task that requires only a few minutes.

While writing the arrangements, we have considered the small hands of children. Each tune is in the first position; most of the notes are on the first three strings; and there are no fingerings that present inordinate technical difficulties.

Conversely, we have sought to avoid a problem that plagues many "easy play" music books; that is, tunes that are all written at the first-week ability level. In my teaching experience, I have found that such books tend to dull rather than inspire the musical intellect of students and teachers alike. Included here is an interesting variety of tunes progressing from very easy to early intermediate. This instructional design avoids the common problem of every tune sounding the same, or nearly the same.

It is recommended that all beginners study the preliminary materials on pages 3 to 9 before attempting to play the first tune.

The Companion Audio

1. Tuning notes: Each mandolin string is sounded on the first track of the companion audio. Tuning the mandolin is explained on page 6.
2. Each audio track begins with count-off clicks.
3. Each tune is recorded twice with guitar accompaniment at a moderate speed (tracks 2-24).
4. The student can play along while listening to mandolin and guitar (stereo); mandolin only (right channel); or guitar accompaniment only (left channel).
5. Listening closely to the audio is an invaluable way to memorize tunes in the least amount of time:
   - Listen to a tune several times before you begin to learn it. Memorize the melody of the tune.
   - Listen to the entire audio often when you are not practicing.
   - Test your memory by humming entire tunes while the audio is playing–and when it is not. Retaining (the sound of) a tune in one's mind promotes quick learning and accuracy in interpretation.
6. If you have trouble playing a tune with the audio, work on the tune some more. Play with the audio again later, after you can play the tune from memory without too many mistakes.
7. All serious students should invest in playback equipment that allows for audio tempo changes and looping of phrases. Both the Amazing Slow Downer (software) and the Superscope audio player perform these functions–and more. Modern equipment helps to maximize the effectiveness of each practice session.

Procedure

The songs are organized approximately by level of difficulty. It is recommended that beginners work through the tunes *more or less* in the order they appear in the book. Players with prior experience can learn the tunes in any order.

Regardless of your level of ability, you may at some point encounter a tune that is too difficult. If this happens, try another tune, and then return to the more challenging tune later.

How to Hold the Mandolin

Parts of the Mandolin

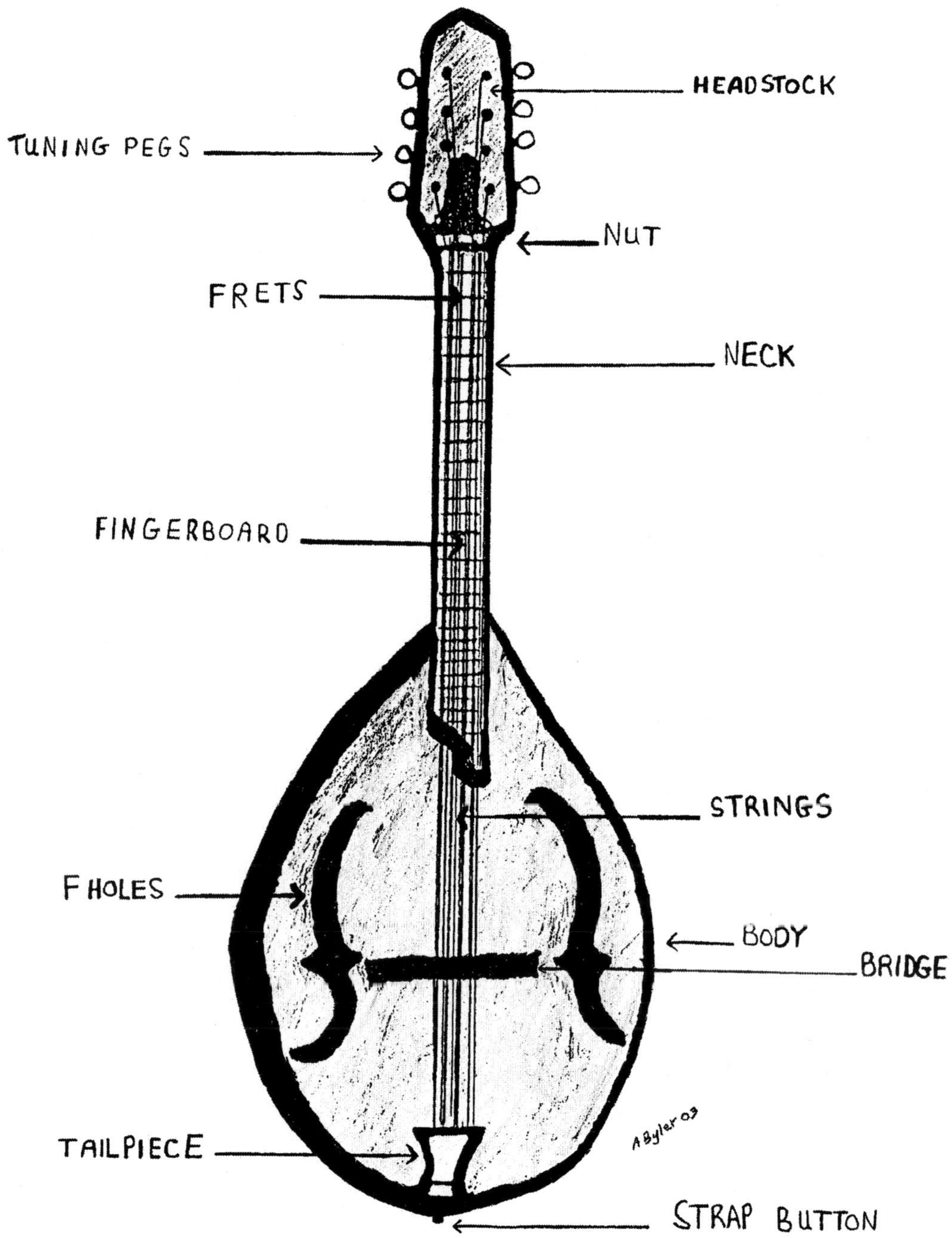

Notes on the Mandolin / Tuning the Mandolin

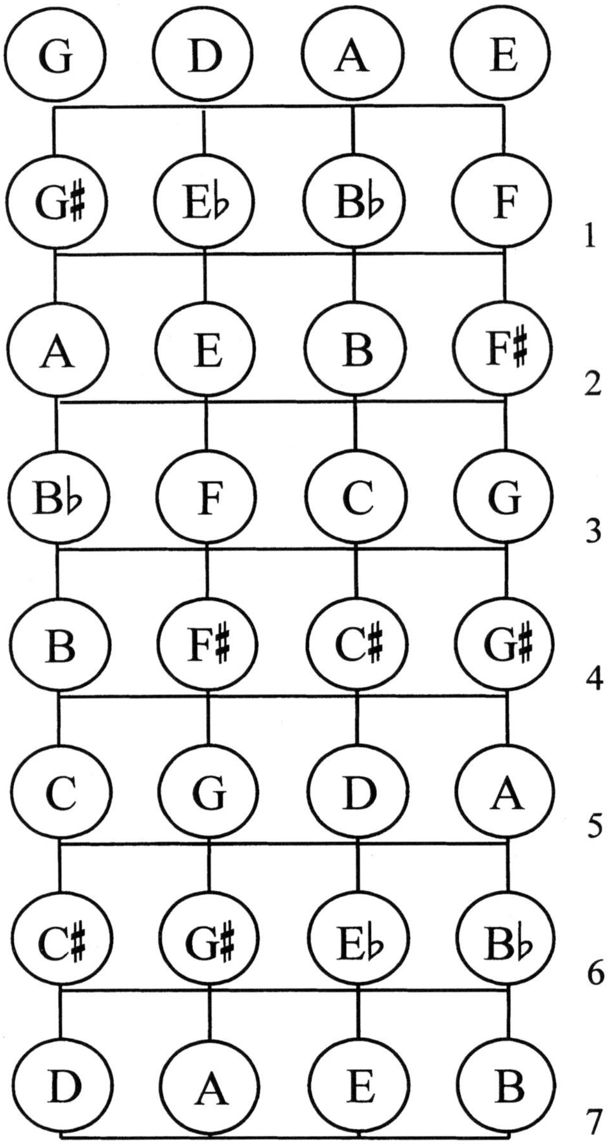

<u>**HOW TO READ THE FINGERBOARD DIAGRAM**</u>

1. The mandolin has four pairs of strings, or eight strings.

2. Each verticle line on the diagram represents a pair of strings. Each pair of strings is tuned the same.

3. The names of the strings appear above the diagram:
   G = The fourth string(s) (the largest in diameter)
   D = The third string(s)
   A = The second string(s)
   E = The first string(s) (the thinnest in diameter)

4. The top horizontal line represents the *nut*. The other horizontal lines represent *frets*. The first seven frets are shown on the diagram.

5. Fret numbers appear alongside the first string.

6. Names of the *notes* appear in circles on the frets.

7. The following examples will help you understand the fingerboard diagram:

- The first string (or string pair) is named E.
- The second fret on the first string(s) is named "F sharp."
- Another F sharp is on fourth fret of the third string(s).
- The note at the first fret of the second string(s) is "B flat."
- Can you name the note on the third string, second fret?

<u>**HOW TO TUNE THE MANDOLIN**</u>

A. The goal is to tune each open string (G, D, A, E) by turning its tuning peg until the string "sounds right."
B. The best way to tune is with an *electronic tuner*, which can be purchased at any music store. Electronic tuners read the vibration of each string and indicate, with a light or a needle, when the string is in tune.
C. An A or E *tuning fork* can be used as an aural reference to tune these strings (A and E).
D. A *pitch pipe* can also be used as an aural reference. However, pitch pipes are never precisely in tune.
E. Each open string can be tuned to its corresponding note on a *piano*.

F. *Relative tuning* (tuning the mandolin to itself) can be accomplished with the following procedure:

1. Tune each E string to its proper pitch. If possible, refer to a piano, tuning fork, or pitch pipe.
2. Tune the second string(s) up or down until the seventh fret sounds the same as the open E string.
3. Tune the third string(s) up or down until the seventh fret sounds the same as the open A string.
4. Tune the fourth string(s) up or down until the seventh fret sounds the same as the open D string.

Music Basics

This information is provided to help tablature readers (page 8) navigate through the measures.

1. Music is written on a horizontal **staff** of five lines (Ex. 1 below.)

2. Mandolin music is written in the **treble clef**.

   • The **treble clef sign** 𝄞 appears at the beginning of the staff (Ex. 1).

3. The lines of the staff are named (from low to high) E G B D F (Ex. 1 and Ex. 2).

   • The four spaces of the staff are named (from low to high) F A C E (Ex. 2).

Ex. 1 The staff has five lines **Ex. 2 Names of the lines and spaces on the staff**

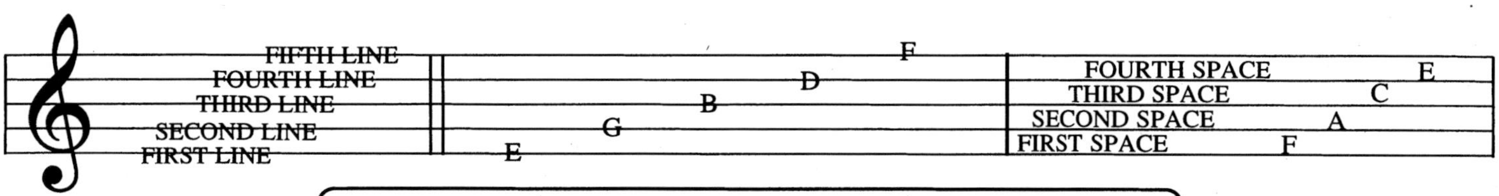

This saying will help you memorize the names of the lines:
Every **G**ood **B**oy **D**oes **F**ine

4. **Bar lines** divide the staff into manageable sections called **measures** (Ex. 3 below).

   • The **double bar** line at the end of Ex. 3. is used to mark the end of song sections (strains).
   • A double bar line is also used to separate examples in music books (Exs. 1 and 2; Exs. 3 and 4, etc.).
   • A "heavy" double bar line (end of Ex. 6) is used to mark the end of a song.

5. The **time signature** (Ex. 4, 5 and 6) shows how many **beats** (counts) there are in each measure.

   • The **4/4** time signature (Ex. 4) indicates four beats in each measure.
   • The **3/4** time signature (Ex. 5) indicates three beats to the measure.
   • The **Cut** time signature (Ex. 6) and also **2/4** (not shown) indicates two beats to the measure.

Ex. 3 Two measures, separated by a bar line **Ex. 4 4/4 time** **Ex. 5 3/4 time** **Ex. 6 Cut time**

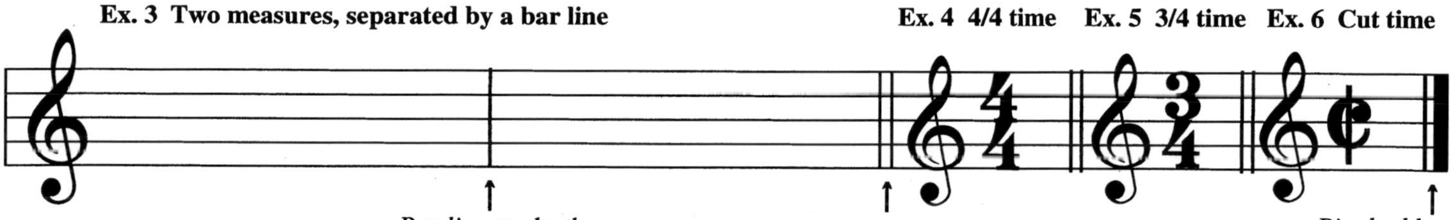

Bar line marks the end of a meausre

Double bar line marks the end of a section

Big double bar line at end of song

Ex. 7 Basic repeat dots **Ex. 8 Repeat between dots** **Ex. 9 First ending** **Ex. 10 Second ending**

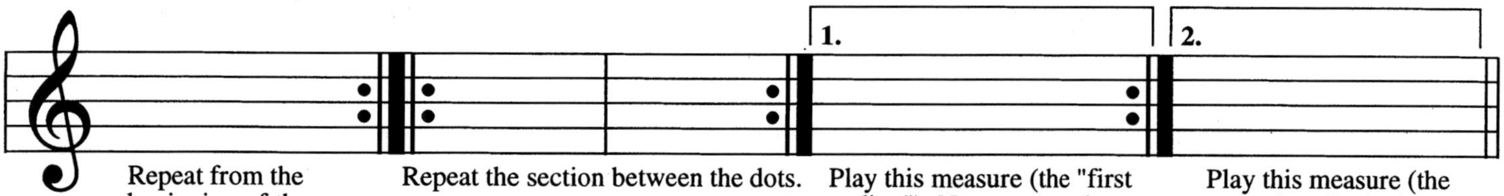

Repeat from the beginning of the section.

Repeat the section between the dots.

Play this measure (the "first ending"). Next, repeat the strain. Then play through the measure that precedes the first ending. Finally, "jump" to the second ending.

Play this measure (the second ending), then proceed to the next section, if there is one.

How to Read Mandolin Tablature

Tablature is an easy-to-learn alternative, or supplement, to standard music notation. The tablature *staff* contains lines and numbers that show the exact location of any note. "Tab" can be easily read by anyone, even those who have no background in music. If you do not read music, you will learn the songs in this book by reading the tablature and listening to the audio recording. Note readers have the option of learning from either the music notation or tablature.

Ex. 1

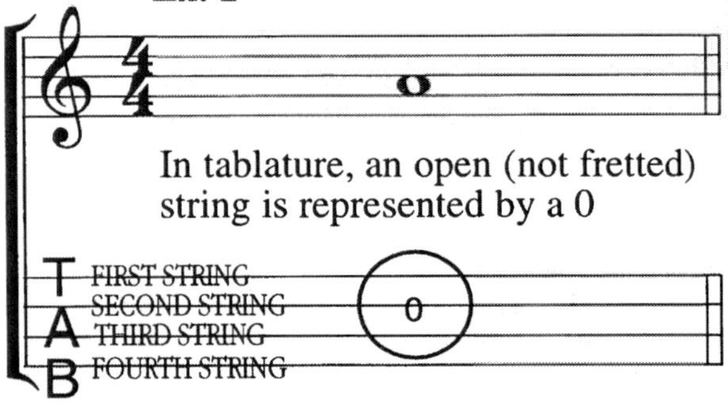

- The top *staff* (Ex. 1-3) is the *music staff*. The music staff, also called the *standard notation* staff, has five lines.
- The *tablature staff* appears below the music staff. This is the staff we are concerned with here.
- The MANDOLIN TABLATURE STAFF has four lines.
- Each horizontal line on the *tab* staff represents a string.

Each pair of strings is considered "a string" in music or tab written for the mandolin.

- The high-sounding string (first string, E) is represented by the top line of the tablature (tab) staff.
- The low-sounding string (fourth string, G) is represented by the bottom line of the tablature staff.
- The tablature in **Ex. 1** tells us to play the the *open* (0) second string. "Open" means a string played with no fingers.

Basic Fingerings for Mandolin

First finger (index) plays first and second frets.

Second finger (middle) plays third and fourth frets.

Third finger (ring) plays fifth and sixth frets.

Fourth finger (little) plays seventh fret.

Ex. 2

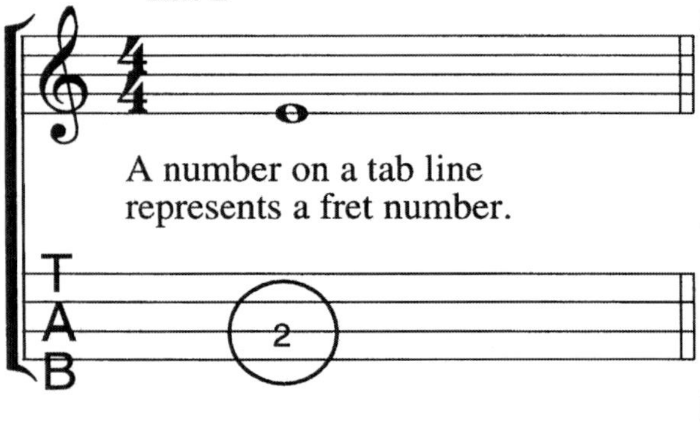

- A *fretted note* is indicated by a number on the tablature staff.
- The note in **Ex. 2** is played at the second fret (2) of the third string. (The first finger usually plays the 2nd fret.)
- The third string is two strings away from the thin string(s), and one string away from the thick string(s).
- The number on the tab staff line shows fret location, not the finger used to play the note.

Ex. 3

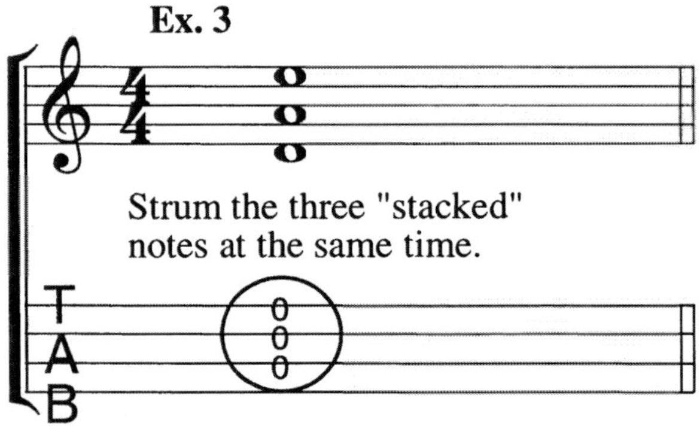

- Sometimes, two or more notes are played at the same time.
- **Ex. 3** tells us to strum three *open strings* (strings 1, 2, 3) together.
- When we play three or more notes at the same time, we are playing a *chord*.

Picking Technique

⊓ *Down-pick symbol*

V *Up-pick symbol*

It is very important to use the proper picking technique when playing the mandolin. The following examples will help you master the essentials of picking.

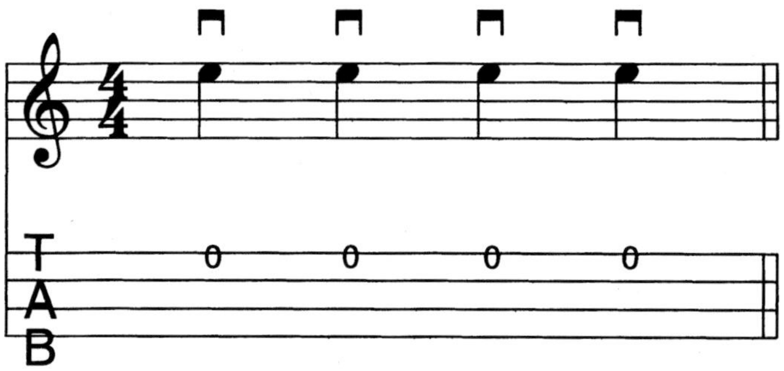

Example 1

Pick each *quarter note* with a down-pick.

Example 2

Each pair of beamed *eighth notes* is picked down, up. This technique is known as *alternate picking*.

Example 3

Picking must be adjusted when both quarter and eighth notes appear in the same phrase.

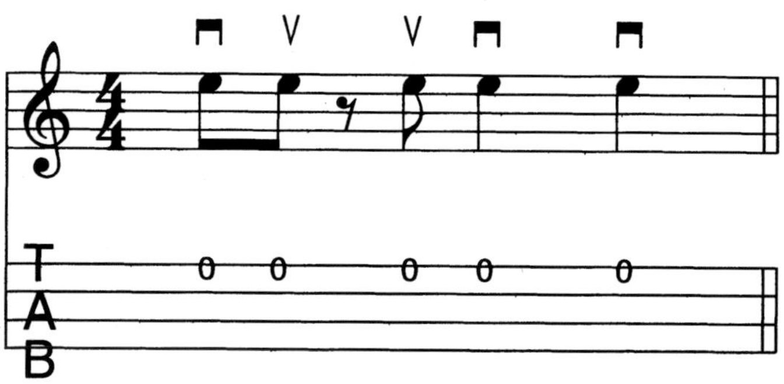

Example 4

An eighth note that follows a downbeat *eighth rest* will be played with an up-pick.

Sweet Betsy from Pike

Pioneer Song, 1851

John Hardy

Outlaw Song

The Sweet Sunny South

Appalachian Song

Reuben and Rachel

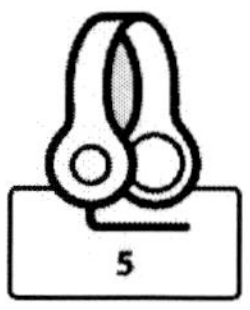

⊓ Pick down
V Pick up

Words by Harry Birch
Music by William Gooch
Comic Song, 1871

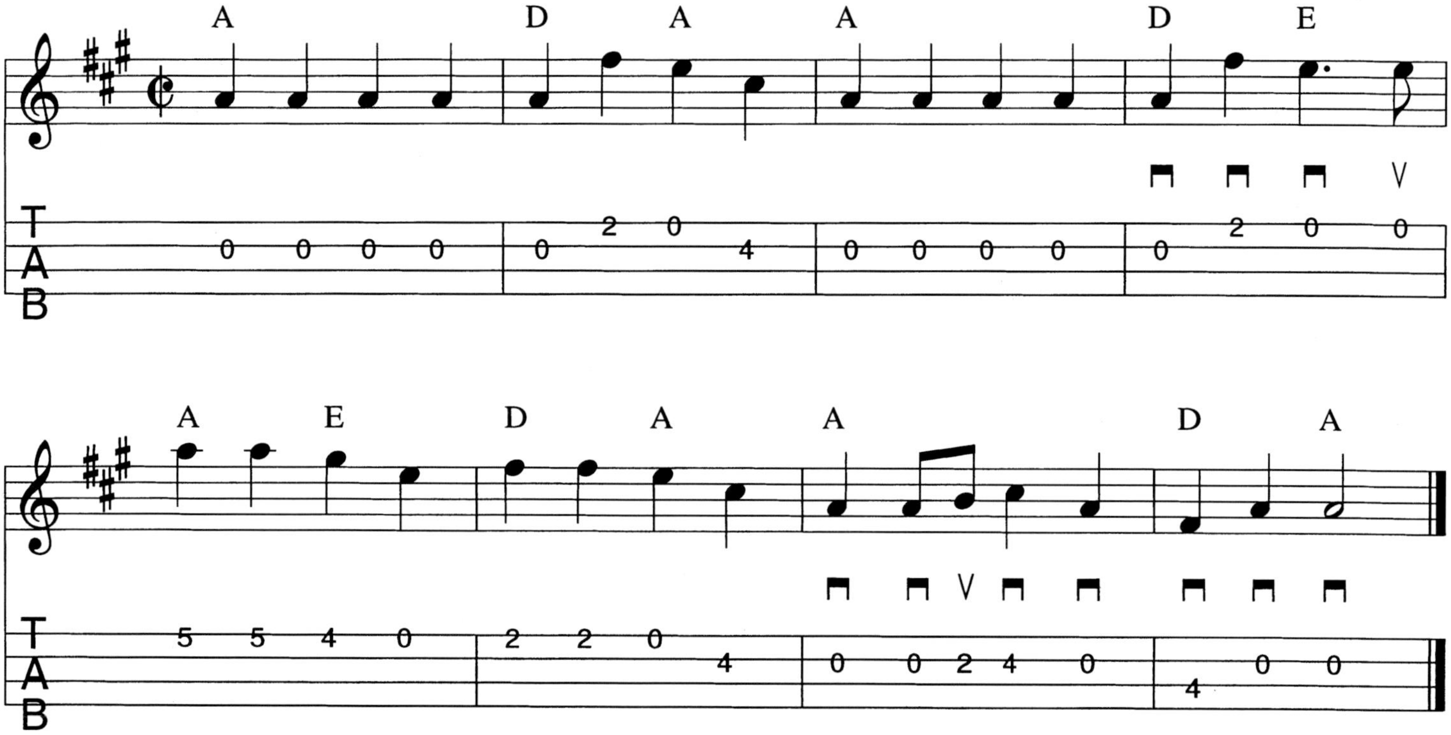

Jack of Diamonds

Traditional

Boil the Cabbage Down

Procedure:
1. Play the first two lines (eight measures). This is the "A" section of the tune.
2. Repeat the first two lines.
3. Play lines three and four. This is the "B" section of the tune.
4. Repeat lines three and four. You have now played the entire tune one time.

Traditional

Salty Dog Blues

Country Ragtime

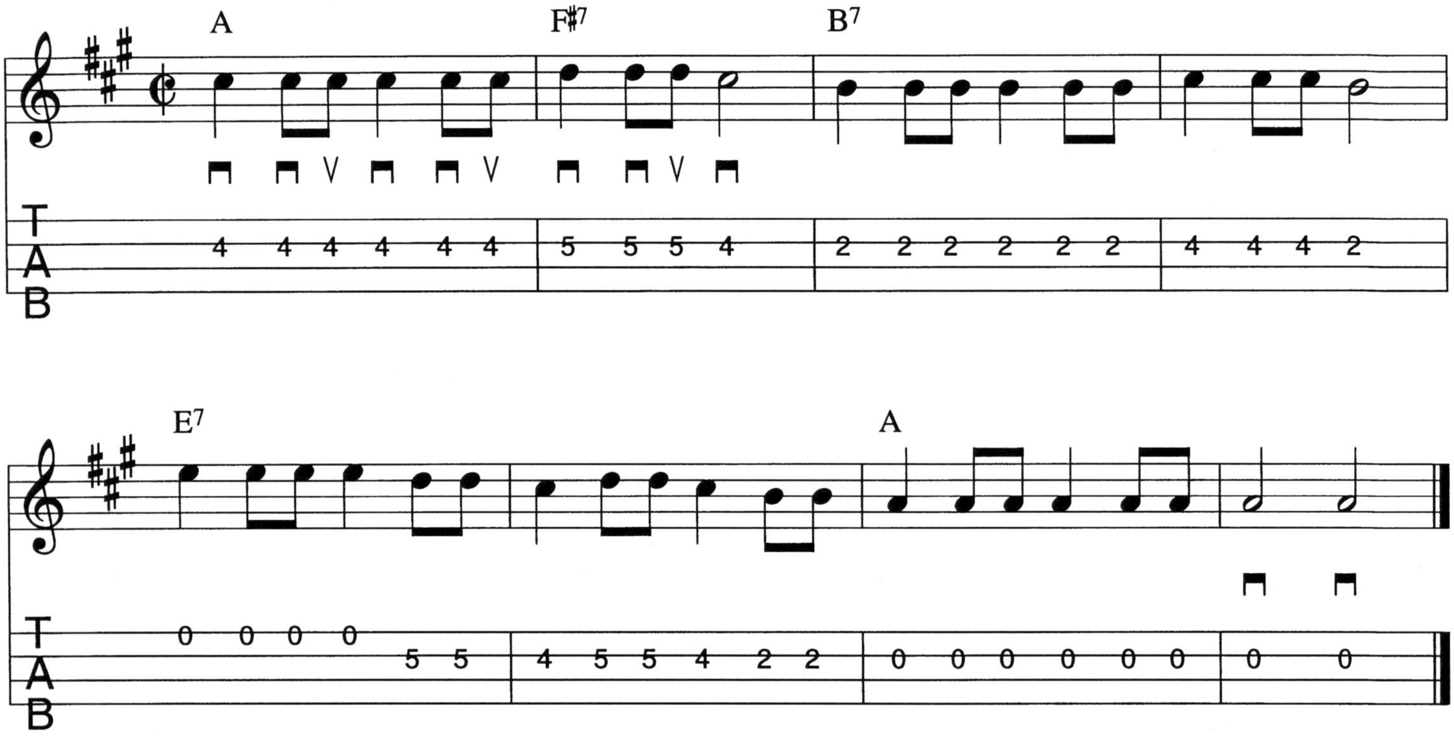

Note: If desired, the guitarist can capo on second fret and play the following chords:

‖ G / / / | E7 / / / | A7 / / / | A7 / / / | D7 / / / | D7 / / / | G / / / | G / / / ‖

Black Eyed Suzie

Old-Time Tune

Colinda

Cajun Tune

The Eighth of January

Old-Time Fiddle Tune

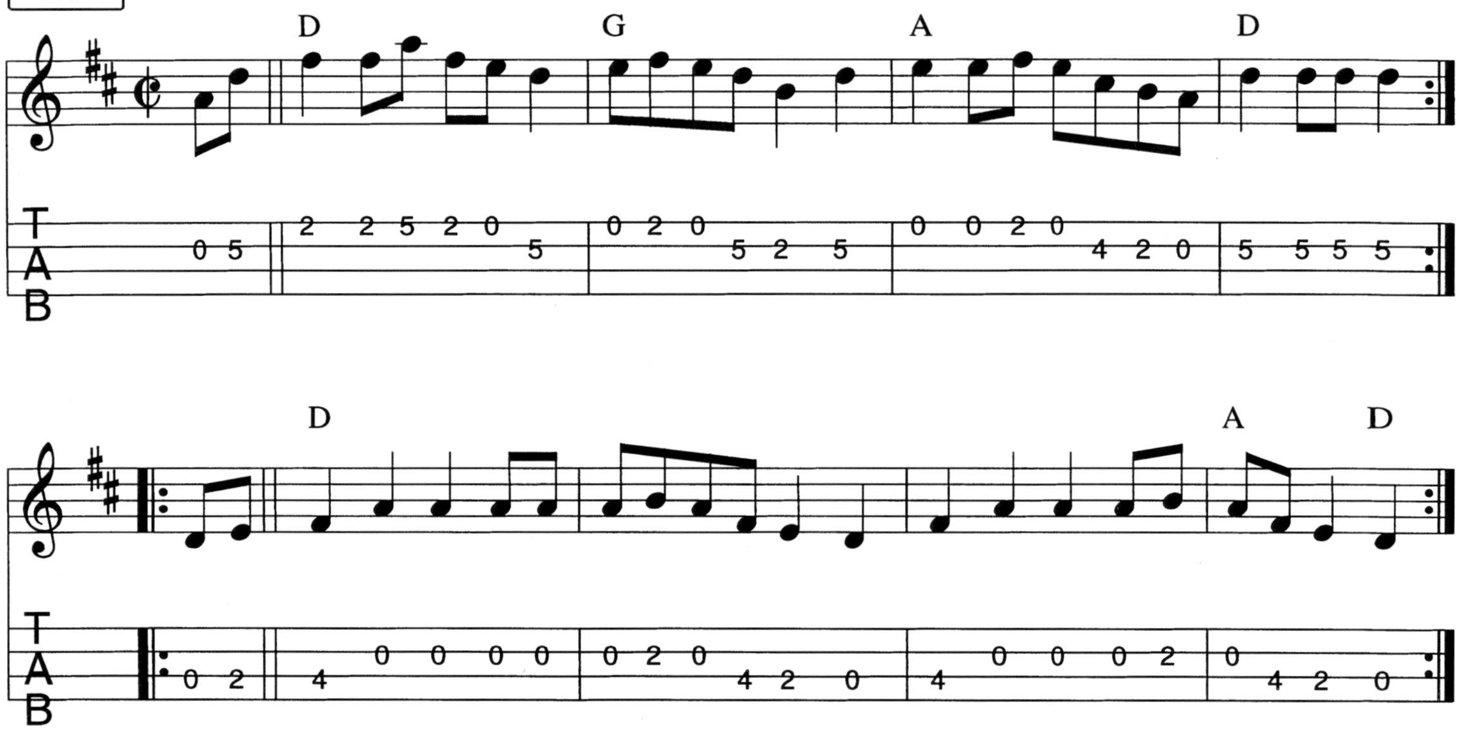

Shortnin' Bread

Minstrel Tune

13

Cripple Creek

Old-Time Song

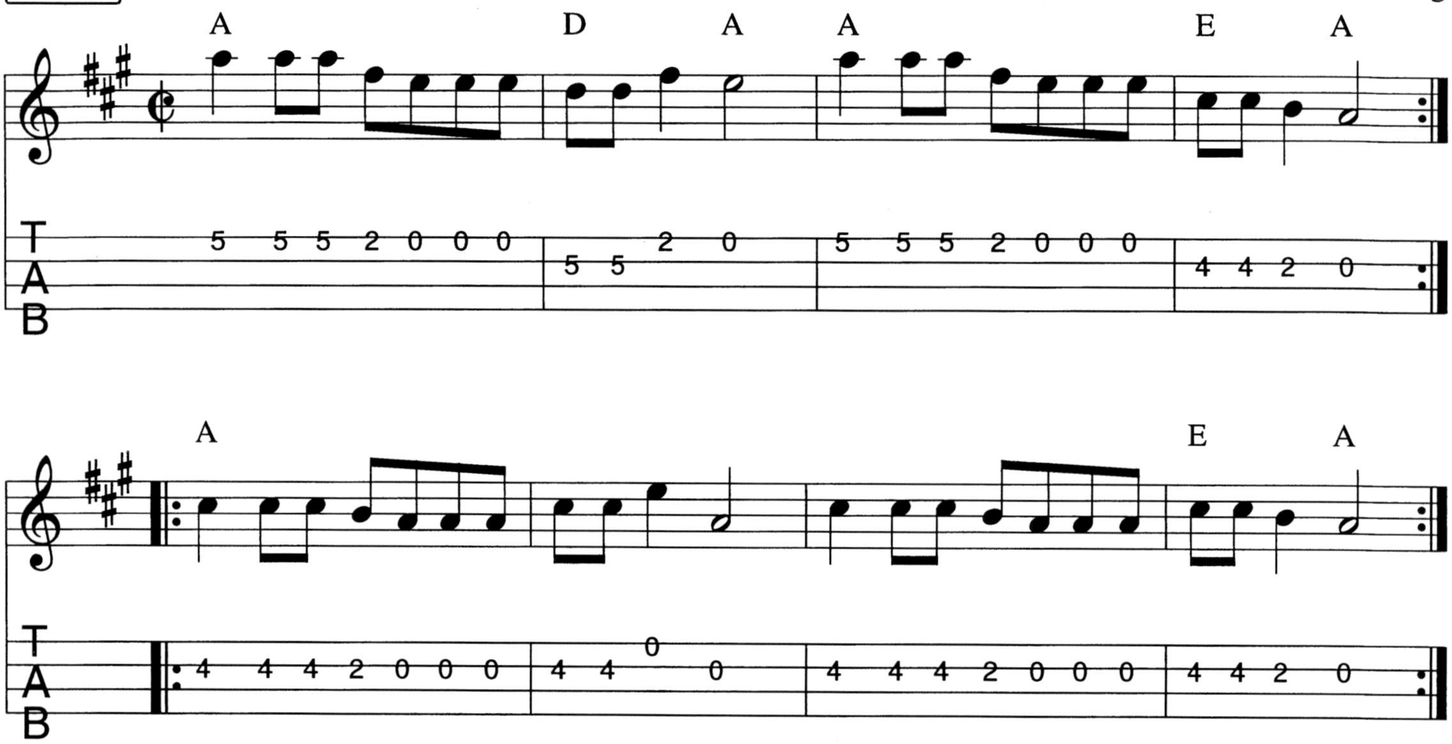

14

Sally Goodin

Traditional Fiddle Tune

Groundhog

Mountain Song

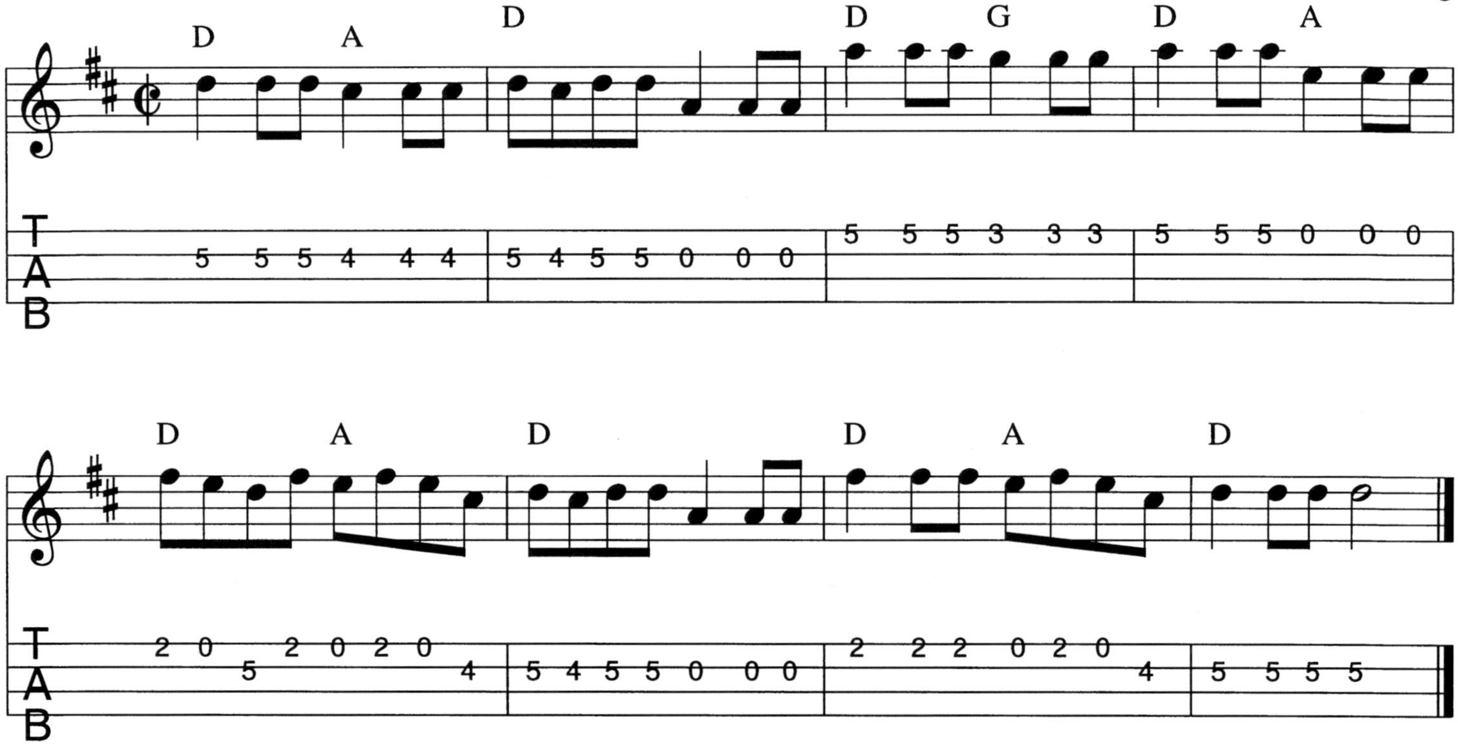

Brigg's Jig

Minstrel Tune

"Brigg's Jig," a minstrel banjo tune composed before the Civil War, is not actually a jig. A "real" jig is in 6/8 time. Minstrel "jigs" are simply lively tunes that are called jigs. This one is still played by many Civil War re-enactment bands.

Steamboat Waltz

19th Century

Fire on the Mountain

Old-Time Tune

Molly Put the Kettle On

Old-Time Song

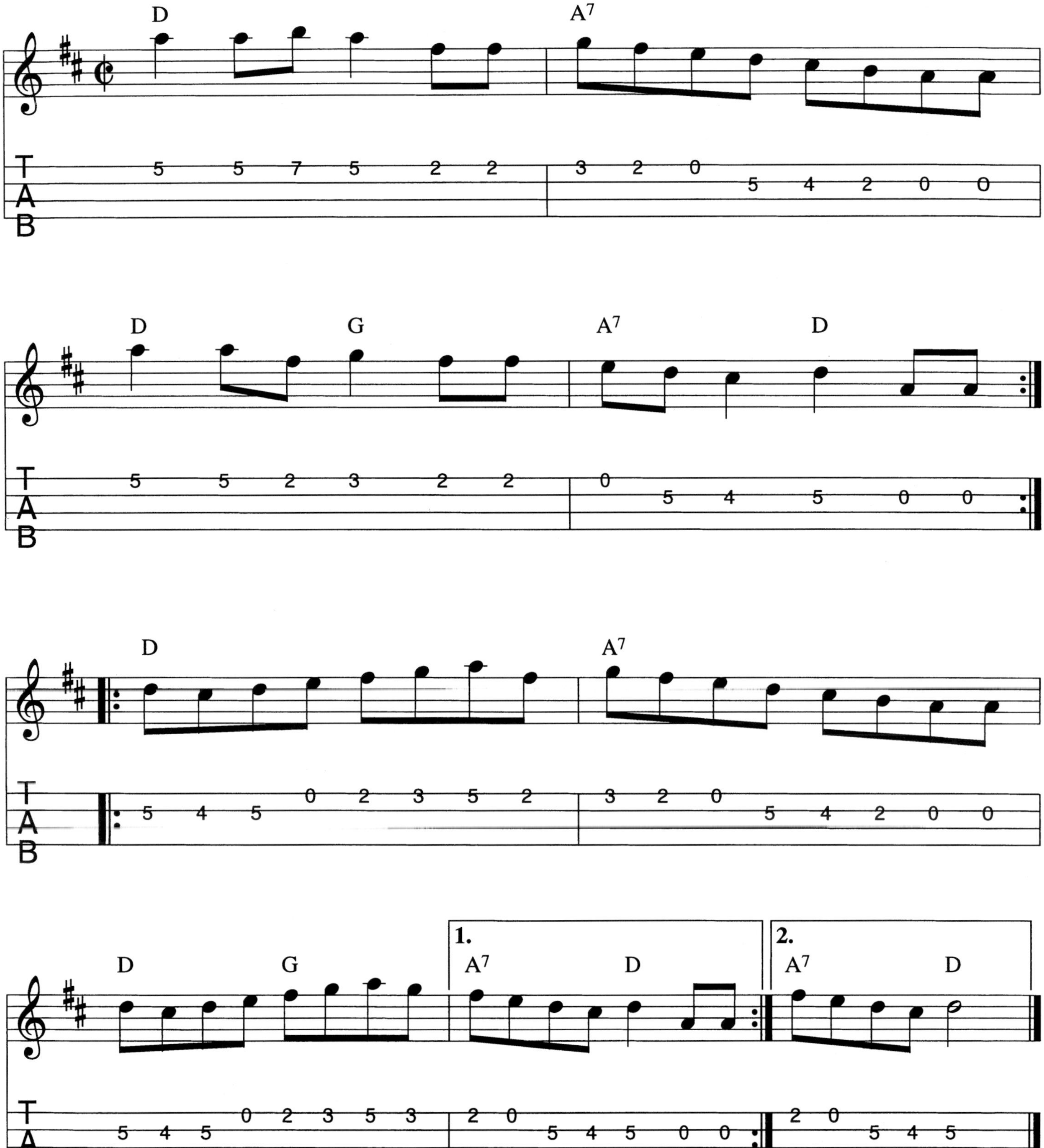

New River Train

Appalachian Song

Red Haired Boy

Traditional Irish Tune

Angeline Baker

Old-Time Fiddle Tune

The White Cockade

English Tune

Slurs

Technique

A *slur* is a technique in which two or more notes are sounded with one stroke of the pick.

Notes comprising a slur have different pitches and are connected in the notation and tablature by either a curved line (Exs. 1-4 below) or an angled straight line (Ex. 5 below).

Examples 1 and 2 below show how to play a *descending slur.* The descending slur is also called a *pull-off.*

How to Play Examples 1 and 2

Example 1:

a) First beat: Place your first finger on the second fret of the first string, then pick the string with a downpick.
b) Second beat: Sound the second string by "pulling" or "snapping" the first finger off the fret.
c) Play the final note in the measure with another downpick.

Remember: The second note is sounded, not with the pick, but by *pulling off* the first finger.

Example 2: This example is played the same as Ex. 1, except the first two notes are on the second string.

Ex. 1 **Ex. 2**

Examples 3 - 5

Example 3 (below) is an *ascending slur.* The ascending slur is also known as a *hammer-on.*

Example 4 contains a pull-off (the first two notes) followed by a hammer-on (the last two notes).

Example 5 shows a *slide:*

1. Fret the second string at the second fret with the first finger.
2. Pick the second string with a downpick.
3. Count one beat, then "slide" or "glide" the first finger from the second fret up to the fourth fret so that the fourth fret sounds on the second beat. Keep finger pressure on the string while executing the slide. Result: Two notes are sounded with one motion of the pick.

Ex. 3 **Ex. 4** **Ex. 5**

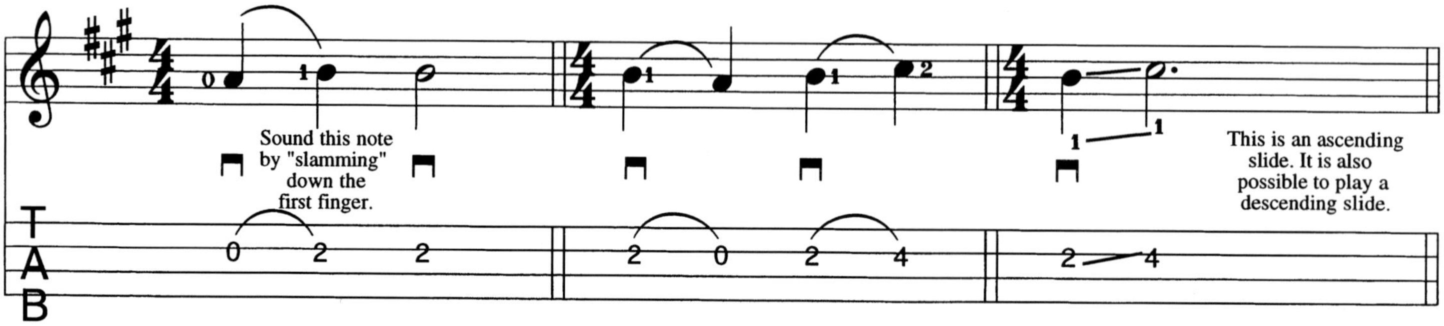

Watermelon on the Vine

Minstrel Song

INDEX OF TUNES